MISFITS

A 31 Day Journey To Revealing

The *Miracle* of YOU!

Black & White

Jessica AA Highsmith

as

ALEX J

THE MIRACLE REVEALED:

A 31 Day Journey to Revealing the Miracle of YOU!

Black & White Version Printed and Published 2021

Copyright © 2018

EMPOWER ME BOOKS, INC.
A Subsidiary of Empower Me Enterprises, Inc.

Illustrations: Saba Abdual Khaliq

Interior Design | Cover Design | Editing
DHBonner Virtual Solutions LLC
www.dhbonner.net

ISBN: 978-1732773196

Printed In The United States Of America

This book is Dedicated to the broken,

the loved, the whole, the un-whole, the one who is unsure

about themselves, the very confident... and the Misfit.

―――――――・⋯⁂⋯・―――――――

I thank God for being the
Author and Finisher of my Faith.
HE is STILL writing my story!

I thank my Family, Friends,
Associates and Colleagues who have
supported the vision in any form.

I thank my church family,
whether past or present, that has
supported the vision God is
birthing through me.

I thank my Mom, Cynthia Alexander,
who was an Angel and Godsend
to change my life.

And, I thank all my readers
forever and always!

Much Love… Grow with Christ!

―――――――・⋯⁂⋯・―――――――

Introduction

————— ·~∿~· —————

We all experience different crosses. My cross included years of childhood rape, abuse, and growing up in foster care.

So, this book was birthed out of the pain of a Misfit and dedicated to evoking inspiration and motivation.

The Misfit series seeks to challenge those who have encountered any type of traumatic experience, to not just survive it, but to overcome it; realizing that God has graced them in such a way, to allow them to have success, despite of the trials of life.

Book One, *Finding my Voice*, was based on experiences and reflections that led to me finding my voice. Book Two, *The Miracle Revealed*, was the revealing of God's foresight, following these experiences.

It really strengthens others to know that no matter what they may have come through, God is able and He is in their corner. He seeks to reveal the miracles of who He has called us to be prior to our birth... to STILL come forth.

Our past, our hurts, and our painful experiences do not render us as damaged goods; but instead, we are the Miracle we yearn for and God has used our life as the Testimony.

Welcome to the 31 Day Journey of Revealing the Miracle of YOU!

.

IN SPITE OF THE EXPERIENCES...

·—◆—✦—◆—·

BUILD STRENGTH

FIND FORGIVENESS

GRAB HOLD TO HOPE

DAYS 1-10

·—◆—✦—◆—·

Begin each morning during this section with 15 Minutes of Prayer, opening up to God, and talking to Him. You can start with writing Letters of your prayers to God and then reading them aloud to Him; if you need to.

Relax; lie or sit before the Lord for 25 minutes listening with your spirit.

During the final 20 minutes, Meditate and Study the Focus Scripture for the Section.

The Work to be completed is intense, but God is waiting for you.

---·⋇·---

SECTION ONE:

---·⋇·---

FOCUS SCRIPTURE
Excerpt from Job 3: 1-26 MSG

"Then Job broke the silence.
He spoke up and cursed his fate:
"Obliterate the day I was born... May God above forget it ever
happened. Erase it from the books!
...it released me from my mother's womb
into a life with so much trouble...

Why didn't I die at birth,
my first breath out of the womb my last?
...Why does God bother giving light to the miserable, why bother
keeping bitter people alive...
What's the point of life when it doesn't make sense? ...when God
blocks all the roads to meaning...
The worst of my fears has come true...
No rest for me, ever –

death has invaded life."

DAY 1

Seeking Man's Approval

*"I do not accept glory from human beings,
but I know you. I know that you do not have
the love of God in your hearts."*

JOHN 5:41-42 NIV

I sought the approval of those around me; struggling to fit into a pre-made, preconceived mold created by others and craving acceptance and intentionally pursuing validation. I began to take inventory of myself, and readily invited those around me to participate as well.

LESSON: Although we may appreciate the positive Godly feedback of others, God should be the only person from whom you seek approval. Have you ever stopped to think that maybe you are inviting people to have front row tickets to the world premier featuring YOUR Life? When you do this, you open the door for their opinions and advice.

Do not put the advice of others, or even your own feelings, before that of His.

REFLECTION

Write down the names of those you seek to impress in your life? Who are these people?

_____

_____

_____

_____

_____

_____

_____

_____

_____

PERSONAL NOTES:

_____

_____

_____

_____

_____

_____

DAY 2

Relinquished Power

"… this is what the Lord says—he who created you, Jacob,
he who formed you, Israel: "Do not fear, for I have redeemed you;
I have summoned you by name; …"

ISAIAH 43:1

I had relinquished ultimate power into the wrong hands; my growth became stagnant in many areas. I would eventually find myself going to the one source, God.

LESSON: The things we go through can cause us to give up the power that God gave us. Sometimes it's just something we may have caused, but for whatever the reason, we have to know that we don't have to stay powerless. Once you gave up your power, or it was taken, you gave up your voice.

REFLECTION 1

Some experience, trauma, or issue has rendered you powerless in a particular area as it pertains to your voice. Start with reflecting on what things you have survived.

REFLECTION 2

Do you consider the things you have survived as victories? Why or why Not?

DAY 3

How am I Wired?

"Who you are is related to where you came from."

~ Dr. Miles Munroe

I shared my experiences in *Misfits: Finding My Voice*, as a helper to accompany you along the path to discovering (or re-discovering) your voice, so that you can become your own advocate.

LESSON: YOU must discover and understand HOW you think and seek to understand HOW you process things concerning yourself. There is a war within to be won first.

PERSONAL NOTES:

REFLECTION 2

How do you feel about yourself? Who or What caused you to feel this way?

REFLECTION 3

How angry, hurt or disappointed are you about those things?

DAY 4

─────·⧓·─────

Why am I Wired this Way?

*"When you're honest with yourself
and honest with God!"*

~ Bishop TD Jakes

─────·⧓·─────

In sharing my past brokenness and lack of confidence in *Misfits: Finding My Voice*, you were able to see how once I started peeling back the layers, I found different fragments of myself; which allowed me to deal with what caused me to lose my voice.

LESSON: Now, you must discover and figure out WHY you think and process things the way you do concerning yourself.

As stated previously, what goes on internally will begin to manifest externally.

PERSONAL NOTES:

_____

_____

_____

_____

_____

● ● ●

REFLECTION

Did you create a pseudo (false) personality for protection to hide your true voice? Or, maybe you created a pseudo (false) personality for protection to create a new voice. Either way, which is it for you and why?

DAY 5

———·✦·———

Regain Power & Strength - Part 1

*"I pray that out of his glorious riches he may strengthen you
with power through his Spirit in your inner being,"*

EPHESIANS 3:16

———·✦·———

There was a point when I realized that I had left my voice
behind... I had either lost my power or given it away. Next, I
became scared and timid in a way.

LESSON: Until you can get real with yourself, ask the deep
questions, and pull back the layers, you will not regain strength.
You cannot come against anything you are not willing to face.

REFLECTION 1

*Reflecting and reviewing **All Your Responses from Day 3 & 4**, Discuss
in writing here what Events left you feeling like Job; empty, Powerless, or
Voiceless in your life.*

REFLECTION 2

Why do you to feel this way?

REFLECTION 3

What caused it?

DAY 6

---·⊱✦⊰·---

Regain Power & Strength - Part II

*"For the Spirit God gave us does not make us timid,
but gives us power, love and self-discipline."*

2 TIMOTHY 1:7

---·⊱✦⊰·---

In finding your voice, you really have to dig deep down and say, *I have a voice because God gave me one. He gave me the power and authority to speak, and to declare and decree a thing to come into existence. Therefore, because I know I need to speak to do this, I must then have a voice.*

LESSON: God's voice, His word, CANNOT return to you void or LIE. So, Satan has to be the one lying to you and filling you with self-filling doubts. You have to hear God, commit to what you heard, and not follow any strange voices that contradict what he said concerning you

REFLECTION

Study the Following Scriptures & write down what they mean to you:

2 CORINTHIANS 12:9

ISAIAH 40:29-31

DAY 7

---·✶·---

Regain Power & Strength - Part III

"Get rid of all bitterness, rage & anger, brawling
& slander, along with every form of malice."

EPHESIANS 4:31

---·✶·---

The things one experiences, sets the tone for the development of not only personality traits, morals and cultural beliefs... but fears, too! We then allow the hurtful issues or trauma to influence who we are, what we are, and who we connect to.

LESSON: Forgive whoever it is you have to, so that you can move forward. *Even if that someone is YOU.* By holding on to all of the pain, you continually cause pain to yourself. You then allow the bitterness to take root; deep, deep roots, which hinder you from finding YOUR voice.

REFLECTION 1

How does bitterness look on you?

REFLECTION 2

How has bitterness poisoned your life?

DAY 8

---·⫞·---

Love You 1st!

"To get wisdom is to love oneself;
to keep understanding is to prosper."

PROVERBS 19:8 NRSV

---·⫞·---

God created you in His image and He is a God of Love. We are admonished biblically to love God with our whole heart, soul, and mind; so, if we are created in His image, then by loving Him 1st, we are equally loving ourselves 1st. *This should be where the "Aha Moment" kicks in.*

God pours wisdom out to those who love Him. If you love God, you will please Him, and if you please Him, then He will give you wisdom [Ecclesiastes 2:26 NIV] God empowers us through the Holy Spirit, and we should speak and think about ourselves in the same way God does.

LESSON: When you begin dealing with how you are wired mentally, you may need help coping with the underlying problems that have caused you to no longer see yourself the way God does. There is no shame in seeking help and support from anointed and certified professionals.

REFLECTION 1

Do you love yourself? What does that Love look like?

_____

_____

_____

_____

_____

_____

_____

_____

_____

_____

_____

REFLECTION 2

What makes you love yourself? Whatever it is, it is a reflection of how you love God.

_____

_____

_____

REFLECTION 3

Do you know God loves you? Can you feel his love for you? His love cannot be earned and it is not based on condition or your experience. Write down all the things you are blaming God for.

_____

_____

_____

_____

_____

_____

_____

_____

_____

_____

_____

_____

REFLECTION 4

Read aloud to God what you just wrote. Although he already knows, HE wants you to verbalize it to him. Talk with him.

DAY 9

---·⋏·---

Conversations with God

*"The Lord would speak to Moses face to face,
as one speaks to a friend."*

EXODUS 33:11a NIV

---·⋏·---

I wanted to know straight from God why I was a Misfit. I wanted to hear from HIM...

LESSON: True, there have been some rough seasons, but there have also been some great and exciting seasons as well.

You have to get to a place where you can hear from Him. Block out the chatter of how people have described you; good or bad.

REFLECTION 1

What have you learned this far about yourself?

_____

_____

_____

_____

REFLECTION 2

Are you willing to use God's strength to give you hope for an expected in; in lieu of the problems, trauma, experiences, or issues?

_____

_____

_____

_____

_____

_____

_____

_____

_____

_____

_____

REFLECTION 3

Tell God Everything You Just wrote in Reflection 2.

DAY 10

---·ᐛ·---

Tired of Being a Rock Badger

*"The rock badgers aren't a strong species either,
yet they build their dens in the rocks!"*

PROVERBS 30:26 ISV

---·ᐛ·---

Like Job, I had lost my voice. And like Job, all strength was lost. Job became silent, and once he did speak, the words spoken were clearly polluted by bitterness and negativity. This WAS NOT HIS VOICE and it was NOT mine.

LESSON: Job's experiences had been allowed to suck what *seemed to be his life* out of him. Although a humble and wise man, one can imagine that with all he was dealing with, he had every right to want to hide and die.

To build your strength, forgive yourself for wanting to give up and for becoming bitter. Exercise forgiveness with whomever you need, so that you can regain your voice through the hope and love God has for you through Christ Jesus.

REFLECTION 1

Go to the Mirror and Repeat the following words aloud:

I pledge to go in God's boldness; even while He is healing me!

I love me!

God loves me and I cannot stay here voiceless or fearful!

Full Circle:

Sometimes, we have to revisit certain stages in life to get to the root of a thing. It will cause you to come full circle; allowing you the chance to be elevated to another level. Finding your voice requires you to get naked.

Naked and Vulnerable.

God wants you naked, vulnerable, and broken in front of Him, so that HE can rebuild you and restore your voice. He wants you to talk to him.

You may have to find your voice at many levels in your life, because we are always growing and being stretched!

REFLECTION 2

Take a moment to re-read all of your entries from these first ten days. What has God Spoken to you in your spirit?

JESUS, THE ONE & ONLY MAJESTIC POWER WHO CAN HEAL YOU. IN HIM, YOU CAN FIND...

ENCOURAGEMENT

PEACE

INSPIRATION

TO OVERCOME, TO STAND BOLD, TO BE COURAGEOUS,

DAYS 11-24

Begin each morning during this section with 25 Min of Prayer. Spend 25 Min Laying Prostrate before the Lord. Use the last 10 Min to Meditate on the scriptural word for this section.

SECTION TWO

FOCUS SCRIPTURE
Excerpt from John 5: 1-7 MSG

"Soon another Feast came around and
Jesus was back in Jerusalem. Near the Sheep Gate
in Jerusalem there was a pool, in Hebrew called Bethesda, with
five alcoves.

Hundreds of sick people—blind, crippled, paralyzed—were in
these alcoves.

One man had been an invalid there for
thirty-eight years. When Jesus saw him stretched out by the pool
and knew how long he had been there, he said, "Do you want to
get well?"

The sick man said, "Sir, when the water is stirred,
I don't have anybody to put me in the pool. By the time I get
there, somebody else is already in."

DAY 11

The Courage to Walk

"Jesus saith unto him,
Rise, take up thy bed, and walk."

JOHN 5:8 KJV

To be healed, and move past simply surviving, you have to get rid of the *woe is me* mentality. Do you really want to be healed? I mean, it seems like that should be common sense, right? But the truth is, often-times we pacify ourselves with our stories; using them as reasons to not get our full deliverance.

This is not saying that the injustice, the pain, or the trauma of what we have experienced was not real. It simply means that it's time to see ourselves the way God created us, and in order to do this we must be healed.

LESSON: The blind man had falling prey to the 'Woe is me' mentality. He started making excuses for why he had not been healed.

REFLECTION

You know your story. Have you been rehearsing it and allowing it to pacify your pity party? Why do you feel like you deserve to be a victim?

DAY 12

---·✦·---

You've Simply Been Surviving

"Yet in all these things
we are more than conquerors and gain
an overwhelming victory through Him who loved us..."

ROMANS 8:37 AMP

---·✦·---

Just as recovering alcoholics must first admit they have a problem, you have to first admit that you believe God had somehow caused all these things to happen to you.

If not that, you will need to admit you have felt that there is absolutely no part you can play in helping yourself recover from whatever your ordeal or story is.

LESSON: Thankfully, when the blind man saw Jesus, he knew to *look* to him for his healing. We can find comfort in doing the same. Jesus paid it all for us before we ever even *thought* to ask.

REFLECTION

You can overcome self-deceit. Yes, you've been lying to yourself. God hasn't lied to you. His word doesn't return void. What lies have you told yourself about taking ownership and responsibility for your healing?

DAY 13

Broken for Much More

"For my yoke is easy, and my burden is light."

Matthew 11:30 KJV

"To grant to those who mourn in Zion…
The oil of joy instead of mourning,"

ISAIAH 61:3 AMP

Most people will only worship God in a time of crisis. When you really want to get God's attention, or His help, you have to do one thing:

Let your brokenness lead you to pure unfiltered worship.

LESSON: There is an innate need built into us that yearns to worship; although many of us run at the first sight of it. When you worship, you cast aside every fear, problem, pain, hurt, or condemnation. God never gave you that weight.

REFLECTION

In what ways do you feel broken? Do feel the urge to cry out to God for healing and deliverance?

DAY 14

·-·✜·-·

Ego Tripping

*"If we walk in the light,
we have fellowship with each other...."*

1 JOHN 1:7 NIV

·-·✜·-·

Sometimes, we can be so hell-bent on our own way. Yes, I said *hell-bent*. There is nothing heavenly sent about it. Just kidding. But seriously, God wants to heal you, but a relationship is a two-way street. He only requires your total adoration. He is a Perfect Gentleman and would never ever force you to do anything.

LESSON: In worship, we come to be vulnerable, and when you've been broken, your Ego tells you that you are fine, and that it's not that deep or it's not that serious.

Oh, but it is! So, stop tripping!

PERSONAL NOTES:

DAY 15

—✧—

Deliverance: Pour Yourself Out

"Trust in him at all times;
… pour out your heart before him:
God is a refuge for us…"

PSALM 62:8 KJV

—✧—

Search for these two songs:

Shekinah Glory: *Yes*
William McDowell: *I Give Myself Away*

REFLECTION

Pour out your spirit before God; the deep things. Pour out to Him. Open up to Him. Let the issues of your heart flow.

DAY 16

---•⚘•---

Day One of Praise

*O my soul, bless God. From head to toe,
I'll bless his holy name! ...God makes everything
come out right; he puts victims back on their feet.*

Psalms 103: 1-18 MSG

---•⚘•---

Let the prayer below simply open the door to your Praise:

Father God, I come to you in prayer to tell you that I think you are wonderful in all of your ways. I come to you right now, asking you to use me as your canvas.

Paint the stroke of humility and service into my mind and heart, God.

[You Continue]...

PERSONAL NOTES:

DAY 17

Day Two of Praise

"Praise be to the Lord, to God our Savior,
who daily bears our burdens."

PSALM 68:19

Continue pouring out your spirit before God. Just as before, let the prayer below simply open the door to your Praise.

Heavenly Father, teach me to relinquish my prideful ways, and show me how to set aside strongholds or wills that were never Yours; that I might go forth on the path that is Your will, God.

Place in my mind a refreshing, a determined heart, and a renewed spirit. Give me a spirit Lord God of joy, peace, hope, faith, love, and long-suffering.

[*You Continue*]...

PERSONAL NOTES:

DAY 18

---·◦ルᵉ·---

Day Three of Praise

"But I will sing of your might;
I will sing aloud of your steadfast love in the morning.
For you have been a fortress for me
and a refuge in the day of my distress.
O my strength, I will sing praises to you,
for you, O God, are my fortress..."

PSALM 59:16-17 NRSV

---·◦ルᵉ·---

Search for these songs:

VaShawn Mitchell: *Chasing After You*
Pastor Charles Jenkins: *My God is Awesome*

REFLECTION

Now that you have been positioning yourself to praise, using your newly found voice, use your praise to open the door to deliverance. Have the courage to set your own atmosphere for healing transformation.

PERSONAL NOTES:

DAY 19

———— ·✦· ————

Deliverance: Purging of the Old

"…if anyone is in Christ, there is a new creation:
everything old has passed away; see, everything has become new!"

2 CORINTHIANS 5:17 NRSV

"The sacrifice acceptable to God is a broken spirit;
a broken and contrite heart, O God, you will not despise."

PSALM 51:17 NRSV

———— ·✦· ————

Search for this song:

Shekinah Glory; featuring Kim Stratton: **Broken**

REFLECTION

Cry out to God as you let him know what you want to be purged of. Ask God for Mercy and Healing. Ask God to remove every stony place and to do heart surgery. It's that serious.

PERSONAL NOTES:

DAY 20

---·✦·---

Basking In His Grace

"The Lord will fight for you,
and you have only to keep still."

EXODUS 14:14 NRSV

---·✦·---

I simply love that God gives us the grace and the mercy needed to walk out our healing and deliverance. The need of deliverance has nothing to do with what we may feel someone has done to us; instead, it removes the chains of bondage and the soul-ties that keep us mentally, spiritually, and physically connected to the pain, trauma, or experiences that have now lead to ungodly roots

As the saying goes, Satan may roar, but our Defender is the LION of JUDAH and He will fight for us.

We need to only be still!

REFLECTION

How has God's grace kept you, placed your mind at ease, and given you an even greater love for our Lord and Savior?

DAY 21

---·◈·---

Day One of Worship

"O God, you are my God, I seek you,
my soul thirsts for you; my flesh faints for you,
as in a dry and weary land where there is no water."

PSALM 63:1 KJV

---·◈·---

Open in Adorations and Worship to God. Let the prayer below simply open the door to your Worship.

Oh God, I bless You today and I worship You in the splendor of Your Holiness. You are the author and finisher of my faith; writing my ending from the beginning. Lord God, You are my Peace, my Love, and my Joy! I come worshipping bolding before You with a spirit of gratitude. I pray that Your Kingdom manifest here in my spirit on earth as You operate in heaven.

I love the bread that You provide so lovingly through Your word; You are sure to provide for my every need. I thank You for Your complete deliverance Lord God; according to the power that You have given me. I raise my voice in triumph and gladness, to be shaped, molded, and even pruned by You. I seek to forever honor and praise Your magnificent name!

[You Continue]...

* * *

PERSONAL NOTES:

DAY 22

---·ᐧᐩᐧ·---

Day Two of Worship

"Ascribe to the Lord the glory of his name;
worship the Lord in holy splendor."

PSALM 29:2 KJV

---·ᐧᐩᐧ·---

Just as on yesterday, open in Adorations and Worship to God, and let the song below simply open the door to your Worship.

Search for this song:

Earnest Pugh: *Rain on Us*

PERSONAL NOTES:

_____

_____

_____

_____

_____

_____

● ● ●

DAY 23

---·∿·---

Day Three of Worship

*"But the hour is coming, and is now here,
when the true worshipers will worship the Father in spirit and truth,
for the Father seeks such as these to worship him. "*

JOHN 4:23 NRSV

---·∿·---

Search for this song:

Bishop William Murphy: *Everlasting God*

REFLECTION

Now that you have been positioning yourself to worship the Lord freely. Use this worship song to enter you into worship.

PERSONAL NOTES:

DAY 24

———— ·⚜· ————

Transitional Shifts

"…Behold, the Lion who is of the tribe of Judah,
the Root of David, has overcome; "

REVELATION 5:5 WEB

———— ·⚜· ————

When you feel the shift, you must shift. It's time to spread your wings and see what God has predestined to manifest pertaining specifically to you! At this point, you should feel refreshed, renewed, and in expectation of knowing and realizing *all* God has said about you!

REFLECTION

WORSHIP IS A LIFE STYLE

- *To learn how to praise and worship in spirit and in truth is to walk in total freedom.*

- *To learn to truly Worship God is to fulfill purpose and to gain supernatural healing.*

- *You are called a chosen and peculiar people. Specific to the Praising and Worshiping of Our Lord, this is the true reason for all the distractions that come as trials, traumas, fears, experiences, etc.*

REFLECTION

Take a moment to re-read all of your entries from these past fourteen days. What has God spoken to you in your spirit?

MIRACLES ARE REVEALED...

ONCE PERSPECTIVE AND VISION ARE RESTORED

REVELATION

MANIFESTATION

RESTORATION

DAYS 25-31

Begin each morning during this section with 30 Min of Prayer; pouring out to God and talking to him as before. Now, you have built up a stamina, if you haven't had one previously for prayer.

Relax; lie or sit before the Lord for 15 min just listening to Him with your spirit. The Last 15 min, Meditate and study the Focus Scripture for the Section.

The Work to be completed is intense, but The Miracle is Predicated on your sight.

SECTION THREE

FOCUS SCRIPTURE
Excerpt from Mark 8:22-26 MSG

"Some people brought a sightless man
and begged Jesus to give him a healing touch…

"…Do you see anything?"
He looked up. "I see men. They look like walking trees."
So Jesus laid hands on his eyes again. The man looked hard and
realized that he had recovered perfect sight, saw everything in
bright, twenty-twenty focus…"

DAY 25

Never Alone

When you pass through the waters, I will be with you;
and when you pass through the rivers, they will not sweep over you.
When you walk through the fire, you will not be burned;
the flames will not set you ablaze.

Isaiah 43:2 NIV

When you look back over your entire being or life, an image begins to take shape; an image and remembrance of the God who was with you in every trial, every tribulation, and every success.

Like the blind man, you couldn't fully see it before.

LESSON: Now, that your vision is restored, you should be able to see it clearly! That is a miracle. *The miracle of sight.* Won't He Do It! I am so excited for you. You could have been misinterpreting your journey because your perspective was all wrong.

REFLECTION

What does your vision look like now? What shapes and forms has it taken on?

DAY 26

A Powerful Majority

"What, then, shall we say in response to these things?
If God is for us, who can be against us?"

ROMANS 8:31 NIV

It is a powerful thing to come to the knowledge of truth that if God is for us, it doesn't matter if even the whole world is against us.

We then have nothing to fear.

LESSON: You have never needed anything more than you needed God. He was, and is, the power source; the keeper you needed, not just to make it through, but to overcome.

He wanted to allow you to see the healing that He already gave you from the beginning.

REFLECTION

What does being whole and restored mean to you? How does it feel?

DAY 27

A Perfect Plan

"For I know the plans I have for you,"
declares the Lord, "plans to prosper you and not to harm you,
plans to give you hope and a future."

JEREMIAH 29:11 NIV

When you finally decided to Give yourself away *freely*, when you decided to Pour all of yourself out, then you could clearly see God's Perfect plan for your life. Although many will begin to get a taste of your testimony, they may not believe it initially… and that's ok.

While they are praying for God to send them help, they may miss their own blessing, because they simply cannot fathom the realization that the manifestation of their miracle may be you..

LESSON: God's plan for our life is ALWAYS bigger than just us. It was never about you anyway. Most of those trials, experiences, pains, or circumstances were for someone else OR to grow and stretch you.

Either way, you have Won because God's Plan is Perfect.

REFLECTION

What has God revealed to you about his Perfect Plan concerning you?

DAY 28

Perfected in Weakness

*"But he said to me, "My grace is sufficient for you,
for my power is made perfect in weakness." Therefore
I will boast all the more gladly about my weaknesses,
so that Christ's power may rest on me."*

II CORINTHIANS 12:9 NIV

Stop thinking of yourself as small. Do not allow fears and trembling creep in to keep you from accomplishing all that God has called you to. God perfects any weakness 'You Think' you have through His strength. You are not timid. You are not hiding anymore. You have emerged from the pits of darkness and ash as a beautiful butterfly. Only God can work such miracles.

LESSON: You are the Miracle, Believe It!

REFLECTION

Can you see the things you once saw as weaknesses, as failures, as scars as trash are all tools by which you can now effect change? Write the manifestation.

DAY 29

---·∿·---

A Perfected View

"And we know that in all things
God works for the good of those who love him,
who have been called according to his purpose."

ROMANS 8:28 NIV

---·∿·---

Think back to the blind man. He was healed the instant Jesus touched him; however, he could only see partially. Much like a stigmatism, his vision was still cloudy or distorted. Yet, he couldn't see anything at all before. It took another, loving encounter with the Lord to not just heal his sight, but to perfect it.

The wonderful truth is that despite it all, God is able to make it all work together for our good... and for His glory. When you remember the fiery trials, sufferings, scars, and wounds of your life, and you see how untouched you are, you will become fully aware that God set you up to come out unbothered, untouched, and not smelling like smoke!

LESSON: It's not good enough to deliver you, God wants to heal and restore you completely in every area of your life, so that your Destiny and Manifested Purpose can come forth, to launch not only your best life but the Kingdom forward.

● ● ●

REFLECTION

What's your Perfect Vision Look like?

DAY 30

Perfected in Love

*"And now these three remain: faith, hope and love.
But the greatest of these is love."*

I CORINTHIANS 13:13 NIV

The funny thing is *Our Love fails*. Why? Because human love chooses when it will enter or exit a commitment. Thankfully, *God's Love never fails*, because He is Committed to us. He is committed whether we are angry, bitter, broken, healed, or restored.

His love committal is not predicated on how He feels in the moment; instead, He labors with us, extends effort, compassion, and energy at a level we could never fully comprehend.

LESSON: It is this *Unfailing Love* that now encompasses and flows through us. You will find that nothing will flow right until you encounter and embrace His Perfect love.

REFLECTION 1

Search for this Song: Jeannie Deal: *God's Love Song to you*

REFLECTION 2

How Does God's Love make you view yourself now? Do you sense his love? Describe it.

Miracles ARE SET APART.

THOSE WHO ARE LIVING, WALKING,

BREATHING *Miracles,*

LIVE LIVES THAT COULD ONLY BE

EXPLAINED BY SUPERNATURAL CAUSES;

Miracles WHICH ARE PECULIAR AND

HANDPICKED BY GOD HIMSELF, BECAUSE

EVERY GOD-CALLED MISFIT IS A

Miracle.

EAGLE ALTITUDE

DAY 31

Mounting Up

"but those who hope in the LORD will renew their strength.
They will soar on wings like eagles; they will run and not grow weary,
they will walk and not be faint."

ISAIAH 40:31 NIV

God cares for His people. The stripes He received at the cross, were specifically borne to allow the miracle of you (and me) to be manifested. When He died, we were healed from the pain of our past and restored to right relationship with Him, ourselves, and others, even before we were born.

Isn't that surreal?

He is such a powerful, loving God, that He wrote not only the end of your 31-Day journey before you were even born, but also your life's outcome. He was so careful to YET and STILL give you the strength to experience all that you have, just so He could reveal the miracle of you, your purpose, and your destiny.

LESSON: A grouping of Eagles is called a Convocation and they don't tend to mix with other birds. When they do engage, they are there to find something to eat and then take off. They also live in dramatic and extreme temperatures; similar to your life experiences.

Now that God Has fed you, given your life meaning, and restored you, Soar! Spread your wings and fly at Eagle Altitude.

YOU ARE THE MIRACLE and It has indeed been REVEALED!

REFLECTION 1

Search for this Song: Tonya Baker: *Miracles*

REFLECTION 2

Reflect on these past 31 days, what do you know have the capacity to do? What miracles have you discovered? What has God Revealed to you?

ALSO AVAILABLE:

MISFITS: Finding My Voice
      (ISBN: 978-1517459109

MISFITS: The Miracle Revealed
      (ISBN: 978-1979991506)

S.T.E.M. 4 Girls: The Urban Girls Guide to the STEM Disciplines
(ISBN: 978-1530231546)

www.ingramcontent.com/pod-product-compliance
Lightning Source LLC
Chambersburg PA
CBHW071832020426
42331CB00007B/1697